I Carry My Mother

I Carry My Mother

For Brenda
and all those you carry —

Lesléa Newman

HEADMISTRESS PRESS

2015

Cover Art © 2014 Carol Marine, *Work Shoes,* 6x6in., oil on panel, carolmarine.com

Cover & book design by Mary Meriam.

PUBLISHER
Headmistress Press
60 Shipview Lane
Sequim, WA 98382
Telephone: 917-428-8312
Email: headmistresspress@gmail.com
Website: headmistresspress.blogspot.com

For my mother, Florence Newman

January 25, 1928 – August 22, 2012

may her memory be a blessing

Contents

write me a book
so my story lives on,
just don't make me read it
till after I'm gone

—my mother, on her deathbed

Prologue: Preparing to Depart

SAFE PASSAGE

My mother is preparing
to depart and will soon set sail
without me. Standing at sea
I keep a close watch

as the gang plank is lowered
the whistle is blasted
the "All Aboard" is called
and my father steers

my mother by the elbow
his spindly legs unsteady
his scrawny arm
slung across her shoulder

which is anchored by the sea
green oxygen tank
that hangs there heavy
as a bag of wet sand.

On deck now, my mother leans
against the rail as she leaves
us in her wake
growing smaller and smaller

waving goodbye
one last time
her fingers fluttering
in the wind like a sail

my father beside me, waving back
his hand opening and closing
like a beacon
all is well all is well

and as we slowly start
to drift apart
and she journeys
toward a new horizon

I stand ashore, one hand
holding onto my hat
the other waving
for all I am worth

and though I am buoyed
by her love
which floats between us
like a lifeline

when she disappears
I taste salt
I come umoored
the waves knock me down

Part One: Stoic as a Stone

THE DEAL

My mother's doctor tells me, *here's the deal*
She's got six months to live, a year at most
His words lodge in my gut, a heavy meal
My mother's doctor tells me, *here's the deal*
I'm very sorry I know how you feel
But keep your chin up, don't give up the ghost
My mother's doctor tells me, *here's the deal*
She's got six months to live, a year at most

My mother once so elegant and slim
Lies bloated, belly swollen as the moon
She mourns the days when she was young and trim
My mother once so elegant and slim
Now fluid fills her body to the brim
Which means she's dying and she's dying soon
My mother once so elegant and slim
Lies bloated, belly swollen as the moon

My father strokes my mother's swollen hand
His broken body bent in half with grief
He stares down at his ancient wedding band
My father strokes my mother's swollen hand
This ending is so far from what they'd planned
His face a wrinkled mask of disbelief
My father strokes my mother's swollen hand
His broken body bent in half with grief

My mother always loved her tiny feet
Her toenails painted candy apple red
Smooth as marble, high-arched, and petite
My mother always loved her tiny feet
But now she hides them underneath a sheet
Two swollen loaves of yeasty unbaked bread
My mother always loved her tiny feet
Her toenails painted candy apple red

My mother points a finger. "Don't you cry.
My life has been terrific until now."
She stares at me till we see eye to eye.
My mother points a finger. "Don't you cry.
You're making it too hard for me to die.
And that I absolutely won't allow."
My mother points a finger. "Don't you cry.
My life has been terrific until now."

And now my mother's started losing weight
She hasn't been this small in thirty years
There was a time when she'd have thought this great
And now my mother's started losing weight
She jokes that she'll become a fashion plate
Her humor fails to hide her growing fears
And now my mother's started losing weight
She hasn't been this small in thirty years

My mother won't admit that she's in pain
Though now and then she gives a fearful moan
Even when she's sweating from the strain
My mother won't admit that she's in pain
I wonder what she thinks she has to gain
From staying strong and stoic as a stone
My mother won't admit that she's in pain
Though now and then she gives a fearful moan

My mother's urine bag has sprung a leak
Yellow liquid puddling on the bed
The second time it's happened in a week
My mother's urine bag has sprung a leak
She gathers all her strength so she can speak
"We'd all be better off if I was dead."
My mother's urine bag has sprung a leak
Yellow liquid puddling on the bed

And now my mother lets her hair go gray
For forty years she's kept it curled and dyed
I never thought I'd live to see the day
And now my mother lets her hair go gray
She asks my father what he has to say
"Now you're sexy *and* you're dignified."
And now my mother lets her hair go gray
For forty years she's kept it curled and dyed

My mother tells me where she hides her jewels
The diamonds that she wore when just a bride
I'm damned if I will cry—I know the rules
My mother tells me where she hides her jewels
A nurse comes in to ask about her stools
I couldn't make this stuff up if I tried
My mother tells me where she hides her jewels
The diamonds that she wore when just a bride

My mother's best friend Pearl has fallen ill
They've known each other over sixty years
There is no cure, no hope, no magic pill
My mother's best friend Pearl has fallen ill
Her heart is broken and will soon grow still
And yet my mother won't allow her tears
My mother's best friend Pearl has fallen ill
They've known each other over sixty years

My mother's name is Faigl, "Little Bird"
And soon she'll spread her wings and fly away
Leaving me behind without a word
My mother's name is Faigl, "Little Bird"
Her voice the very first I ever heard
Oh how on earth will I survive that day?
My mother's name is Faigl, "Little Bird"
And soon she'll spread her wings and fly away

And now my father's heart is full of hope
My mother's had two good days in a row
He clings to her, their hands a twisted rope
And now my father's heart is full of hope
And I, the daughter, clueless how to cope
While deep inside, my mother's tumors grow
And now my father's heart is full of hope
My mother's had two good days in a row

At last it is my mother's final hour
No more second chances. No reprieve.
The stench of death is bitter, sharp, and sour
At last it is my mother's final hour
My father has lost every ounce of power
He wipes his runny nose upon his sleeve
At last it is my mother's final hour
No more second chances. No reprieve.

She was just here and now she's just gone
In a New York minute I lost my mother
How can the rest of the world carry on?
She was just here and now she's just gone
On whose loving breast will my head rest upon?
I'll search all my life but I won't find another
She was just here and now she's just gone
In a New York minute I lost my mother

Part Two: Alive and Not Alive

THIRTEEN WAYS OF LOOKING AT MY MOTHER

I
Among seven silent rooms
in the middle of the night
the only moving thing
is a swirl of smoke
rising from the lit tip
of my mother's cigarette

II
My mother was of three minds
like the three sorry children
she would someday come to bear

III
My mother whirled through the kitchen
slamming drawers, banging dishes
clanging pots and pans
She was a noisy part of the pantomime

IV
My mother and her mother
are one
My mother and her mother and her daughter
are one

V
I do not know which I dread more
arriving at my mother's house
or leaving it
The pain of being with her
or the pain of being without her

VI
Knitting needles click and clack
as something wooly grows
My mother stares at her creation
Her mood is indecipherable

VII
Oh skinny blonde airbrushed models
staring up at my mother as she flips
through glossy magazines,
Why must you torture her so?

VIII
I know how to make matzo balls
big as fists
and how to live on nothing
but cottage cheese, cigarettes, and air
but I know, too
that my mother is involved
in everything I know

IX
When my mother moved
from Brooklyn to Long Island
she marked the edge
of one of many circles

X
At the sight of my mother
staring back at me
at three in the morning
from the unforgiving bathroom mirror
I cry out sharply

XI
I rode home on the train
and fear pierced me
in that I mistook
the phlegmy hacking cough
coming from three rows back
for the sound of my mother

XII
The ventilator is on
My mother must be breathing

XIII
It was twilight all day
and all night long
she was breathing
and she was trying to breathe
my mother lay in the ICU
her hand in mine
holding on for dear life

A DAUGHTER'S A DAUGHTER

My mother declares in her hospital room
That my fate was decided deep down in her womb.
A son is a son until he takes a wife,
A daughter's a daughter for all of her life.

She's telling me I am in charge of her fate,
While both of my brothers are deemed second rate.
As she's borne unto death, I will be her midwife
A daughter's a daughter for all of her life.

I argue, I reason, I try as I might,
I learned from the best how to put up a fight.
My mother and I are no strangers to strife,
A daughter's a daughter for all of her life.

The papers are signed, I'm to do as she's said,
If she cannot be cured, she would rather be dead.
Can I cut the cord of her life with a knife?
A daughter's a daughter for all of her life.

MY MOTHER IS

Angry at God for her terrible suffering
Bitter because no one knows how to save her
Cold all the time even under three blankets
Dead set on living as long as she's able
Eager to have all this over and done with
Frightened to die though she'll never admit it
Grumpy from pain that she says feels like labor
Hungry for foods she can no longer stomach
Insisting she's fine and needs no one to help her
Joylessly sipping the juice that I serve her
Kinked up from sitting for hours and hours
Longing to smoke cigarettes like she used to
Mourning her life which is fast disappearing
Nervous she'll drop dead with no one beside her
Offended whenever I use the word hospice
Pissed off she needs help to go to the bathroom
Quiet whenever I tell her I love her
Refusing her pain meds for fear of addiction
Scornful of doctors who say not to worry
Trying to make it through just one last summer
Unhinged at the thought of forsaking my father
Vain even now, eighty-four years and counting
Weary of being a burden to others
X-ing out names of dead friends in her phone book
Yearning to be with her mother in heaven
Zeroing in on her day of departure

MY MOTHER KNITS

My mother knits a fuzzy pair
Of woolen socks for me to wear
The rocker creaking as she rocks
Her knitting needles tick like clocks
She doesn't have much time to spare

Her body in such disrepair
She's grown as thin and light as air
Death sniffing round her like a fox
My mother knits

She claims the root of her despair
Is simply that my feet are bare.
And so she knits and purls and blocks
Determined to cast off these socks
Before Death drags her to His lair,
My mother knits

MY MOTHER LIVES

My mother lives through one more night
Refusing to give up the fight
To die in her mind is to fail
And though her ship is set to sail
She grits her teeth and holds on tight

I wonder when she'll see the light
To suffer so just isn't right
I plead with God to no avail
My mother lives

For two long years this sorry plight
Has been her lot, no end in sight
She's grown so withered, weak, and frail
Her life so far beyond the pale
Yet holding fast with all her might
My mother lives

PRECIOUS MOTHER

The daughter's heart aches, the daughter's heart breaks
As she wakes and takes care of her mother.

Heavy with dread, she creeps to the bed,
Is she dead, or is she my mother?

Hands cold as stone, she feels all alone
Sitting bone to bone with her mother.

Eyes full of tears, mind full of fears,
How to get through the years without mother?

The months have been rough, and though she's been tough,
Enough is enough for a mother.

This much is clear, the time's drawing near.
Is there anything dear as a mother?

Her face thin and frail, her life growing stale,
Her body a jail for the mother.

Will her suffering cease? Will she ever know peace?
Can she bear to release her own mother?

Too frail to speak, so withered and weak,
The future looks bleak for a mother.

Though hope is long past, the daughter clings fast
to what's left of the last of her mother.

Moon rising high, the daughter must try
to whisper goodbye to her mother.

Stars shining bright, her mother takes flight
Godspeed and goodnight, precious mother

SOON

On that day
that unavoidable inevitable
necessary day

that is rushing toward me
on its pure white steed

every letter
of every word
of every language

ever whispered or shouted
spoken or sung

will collide
in my throat
clanging banging

smashing crashing
into one great chaotic cacophonic

yowling howl
that will resound
around the world

and then, then
the empty cradle of silence

will descend
and I will be left
bereft

of the sound
that astounded me

the day I was born
the first sound
I ever heard

a single word
that might have been

my name or a prayer
or the most important thing
I ever hope to hear

the melody of my mother's voice
ringing my tender ear

PILLS

One pill
two pills
red pills
blue pills

three pills
four pills
less pills
more pills

pills to help her take a crap
pills to help her take a nap
pills to ease her aching back
pills that make her stools turn black

new pills
old pills
pink pills
gold pills

square pills
round pills
crushed pills
downed pills

pills so that her blood won't clot
pills so that her brain won't rot
pills to only take with food
pills to change her rotten mood

day pills
night pills
black pills
white pills

big pills
small pills
hard pills
all pills

pills that make her stomach churn
pills that make her insides burn
pills that make her ask me why
she has no pill to help her die

WHEN THINGS FALL APART

She pukes
She shits
She moans
She groans
She gasps
She bleeds

She bleeds
She pukes
She gasps
She shits
She groans
She moans

She moans
She bleeds
She groans
She pukes
She shits
She gasps

She gasps
She moans
She shits
She bleeds
She pukes
She groans

She groans
She gasps
She pukes
She moans
She bleeds
She shits

She shits
She groans
She bleeds
She gasps
She moans
She pukes

Puking, shitting,
moaning, groaning,
gasping, bleeding, she weeps

IN THE ICU

my mother is awake and not awake
my mother is asleep and not asleep
my mother is alive and not alive

the clock is moving and not moving
the monitor is beeping and not beeping
the nurse is coming and not coming

time is passing and not passing

my mother is seeing and not seeing
my mother is hearing and not hearing
my mother is breathing and not breathing

I am seeing her face and not seeing her face
I am hearing her voice and not hearing her voice
I am squeezing her hand and not squeezing her hand

I am beside her and beside myself

I am an orphan and I am not an orphan
I am a daughter and I am not a daughter
I am a child and I am not a child

her daughter
her child

ONCE

Once my mother pushed my stroller
Now I push my mother's wheelchair

Once my mother fed me ice cream
Now I feed my mother ice chips

Once my mother wore evening gowns
Now my mother wears hospital gowns

Once my mother danced all night
Now my mother vomits all night

Once my mother dyed her hair black
Now my mother's urine is black

Once my mother watched *Jeopardy* each night
Now my mother is in jeopardy each night

Once my mother was dying to live
Now my mother is dying to die

IT'S TIME

My mother pale and frail and old
Her hands and feet so blue and cold
She looks at me with one dark eye
"It's time," she says, "for me to die."

I know her life's a bitter pill.
I know this has been coming. Still,
how on earth to say goodbye?
"It's time," she says, "for me to die."

"It's time," she says, "for you to live.
You've given all you've got to give.
Just promise me that you won't cry.
It's time," she says, "for me to die."

She lays her hand upon my face.
My shattered heart begins to race.
My cheeks are anything but dry.
"It's time," she says, "for me to die."

She turns from me and whispers, "Go,"
Her breath as soft and still as snow.
Her final words a whispered sigh.
"It's time" she says, "for me to die."

PARTING GIFT

Plain
size 4
solid gold
worn wedding ring
most prized possession
for more than sixty years
yanked off her swollen finger
and slipped onto a braided chain
now resting against my hammered heart
to have and to hold, till death do us part

HOSPICE HAIKU

Blazing August sun
Heating up hospice window
Inside cold as glass

Mother is sleeping
Inhaling, exhaling,
Breath precious as gold

No food for two weeks
No water for seven days
Kept alive by love

Eyes flutter open
Will she utter one last word?
"Mom?" Eyes flutter closed

Face mottled and gray
Hands and feet blue and bloated
Are you my mother?

Oxygen turned off
That incessant hissing stilled
Room silent as death

BEATEN

My mother, shriveled, shrunken, gray
lies motionless upon the bed
a tiny, mottled lump of clay

she looks like she's already dead
her hands and feet so blue and cold
her bloodless lips no longer red

her wedding ring of tarnished gold
long banished from her waxy hand
too curled and stiff for me to hold

she lies in wait for God's command
to leave us for the world to come
that fabled, perfect, promised land

and I, so hollowed out and numb
sit still beside her standing guard
my heart a beaten, battered drum

my life, like hers, a broken shard

HOW TO WATCH YOUR MOTHER DIE

Push open the door.
Push yourself into your mother's hospice room.
Say, "Good morning, Mom."
Sit down on a cold folding chair.
Cross your right leg over your left.
Cross your arms over your chest.
Slouch.
Sigh.
Stare at her face.
Notice how tiny she looks.
Notice how gray she looks.
Notice how still she looks.
Leap up.
Feel her forehead.
Thank God that it is still warm.
Remember how your mother used to feel your forehead
with the back of her hand when you told her you didn't feel
good.
Say, "Mommy, I don't feel good."
Wait for her to say something.
Listen to her say   nothing.
Sit down on the cold folding chair.
Cross your right leg over your left.
Fold your arms over your chest.
Slouch.
Sigh.
Hear your stomach rumble.
Try to ignore your hunger.
Think: who could eat at a time like this?

Hear your mother's voice in your head:
Don't be silly. Go eat something. I'll be fine.
Ponder what to eat.
Long for the vegetarian chopped liver
she always made just for you.
Realize you'll never eat it again.
Kick yourself for not asking her for the recipe.
Know that even if you had the recipe, it wouldn't taste the same.
Decide that all you can stomach is a cup of tea.
Unfold your arms.
Uncross your legs.
Stand.
Say to your mother, "Don't go anywhere. I'll be right back."
Think how unfunny this is.
Tiptoe out of the room so you don't wake your mother up.
Think about how much you want to wake your mother up.
Think about how much you want to hear her voice again.
Refuse to believe that you will never hear her voice again.
Walk out of the room.
Notice the sun streaming through the large window in the hall.
Quicken your pace.
Feel lighter.
Feel alive.
Feel guilty.
Arrive at the kitchen area.
Pour hot water into a styrofoam cup.
Add a teabag.
Push the teabag down with a white plastic spoon.

Remember that your mother always added
three ice cubes to her tea.
Remember how she loved telling you about the time
she did this in England.
Remember how she loved imitating the utterly appalled waiter:
My dear, you're diluting the tea!
Smile.
Open the freezer and put three ice cubes into your tea.
Watch them bob to the surface.
Watch them disappear.
Drag yourself back to your mother's room.
Enter.
Say, "Hi Mom. I'm back."
Look at the clock.
See that it is only five past seven.
Know it is going to be a very long day.
Wonder how many days you are going to spend like this.
Put your tea on the windowsill.
Sit down on the cold folding chair.
Cross your right leg over your left.
Cross your arms over your chest.
Slouch.
Sigh.
Do not touch your tea.

PRAYER

Go gentle, Mother, into that good night,
Embrace, embrace the dying of the light.

VIGIL

May she go easy
May she go swift
May she not tremble
As things start to shift

May she go gentle
as sweet summer rain
May she be free
Of her heart wrenching pain

May she go calm
As the moon in the sky
Beaming above us
May she not cry

May she go quick
As a thief in the night
May she believe that
We'll all be all right

May she go free
As a bird that has flown
With joy from the nest
To test waters unknown

May she go light
May her burdens release
May she grieve nothing
May she know peace

May she go soft
As a blanket of snow
May she go easy
May she let go

HOW TO WATCH YOUR FATHER
WATCH YOUR MOTHER DIE

Sit beside him on a folding chair beside your mother's bed.
Place a box of tissues between you.
See how he takes your mother's hand in both his own
and strokes it like a small wounded animal.
Do not speak.
Do not turn on the TV.
Do not shatter the silence around you.
Let time pass.
Listen to your father sigh.
Listen to your father sob.
Hand your father a tissue whenever necessary.
Ask your father if he wants something to eat.
Ask your father if he wants something to drink.
Ask your father if he wants to go for a walk.
Do not press him when he says no to everything.
Remember the one thing he wants is impossible to give him.
Let more time pass.
When your father gets up to go to the bathroom and says,
"Hold Mom's hand," hold your mother's hand.
When he returns, give your mother's hand back to your father.
It belongs to him.
Do not tell your father what the hospice nurse told you:
you need to let go so she can let go.
When the sun sets, gather the darkened room
around your shoulders like a cloak.
Watch your father's undying love
take your mother's breath away.

THE PROBLEM

Multiply:
2 packs of cigarettes a day
by 7 days a week
for 52 weeks a year
for 69 years

and what do you get?

one-million-four-thousand-six-hundred-forty
nonfiltered Chesterfield Kings
and one smoldering mother

gone up in smoke

Part Three: Quiet as a Grave

LETTER FROM MOM, POSTMARKED HEAVEN

This is just to say
I'm sorry
I left
you
bereft
and alone

Forgive me
for being a daughter
like you
I always rush off
when my mother calls
come home

LOOKING AT HER

Yes, I was looking at her
Yes, I knew her very well
Yes, I had lived inside of her
Yes, I had lived outside of her
Yes, she had fed me and clothed me
Yes, she had rocked me and soothed me
Yes, I had brought her much pleasure
Yes, I had brought her much pain
Yes, we had fought with great fury
Yes, we had kissed and made up
Yes, I had moved far away from her
Yes, I remained very close to her
Yes, that day I was looking at her
Yes, she was stiff and unmoving
Yes, she was dressed in a shroud
Yes, her two lips stitched together
Yes, her two eyelids sewn shut
Yes, I bent over her casket
Yes, I applied her pink lipstick
Yes, I brushed blush on her cheekbones
Yes, the farewell the departure
Yes, the silence the longing
Yes, I was with and without her
Yes, I was looking at her

HOW TO BURY YOUR MOTHER

Slip out of the dark limo
into the bright light of day
the way you once slipped
out of your mother:
blinking, surprised, teary-eyed.
Turn to your father
and let him take the crook of your arm
like the crooked old man
you never thought he'd become.
Feel your heels sink into the earth
with every sorry step you take.
Weave your way through the graves
of strangers who will keep your mother
company forever: the Greenblatts,
the Goldbergs, the Shapiros, the Steins.
Stop at a small mountain of dirt
next to a hole that holds the plain pine box
that holds what's left of your mother.
Listen to the rabbi mumble
prayers you've heard a hundred times
but this time offer no comfort.
Smell the sweet honeysuckle breeze
that is making your stomach buckle.
Feel the sun bake your little black dress.
Wait for the rabbi to close
his little black book.
Bring your father close to the earth
that is waiting to blanket your mother.
Watch him shove the shovel

into the mound upside down
showing the world how distasteful
this last task is.
See him dump clumps of soil
onto your mother's casket.
Hear the dull thuds
of your heart thunking against your chest.
Watch how your father plants the shovel
into the silent pile of dirt
and then shuffles off
slumped over like a man
who finally admits defeat.
Step up to the mound.
Grasp the shovel firmly.
Lift it up and feel the warm wood
between your two damp hands.
Jab the shovel into the soil.
Toss the hard brown lumps
into that dark gaping hole.
Hear the dirt rain down upon your mother.
Surrender
the shovel to your brother.
Drag yourself away.
Do not look back.

MY MOTHER HAS MY HEART

My mother has my heart and I have hers,
We traded on the day that she gave birth.
Each passing year the line between us blurs,
Until the day I lay her in the earth.
My heart in her now cracked and split in two,
Her heart in me now wound down like a clock,
As she and I turn into something new,
The love between us hardens into rock.
My heart in her a newborn mourning dove,
Still safely tucked inside its sheltered nest.
Her heart in me a letter signed with love,
A treasure I keep deep within my chest.
From this day forth whatever else occurs,
My mother has my heart and I have hers.

AFTER THE FUNERAL

Everyone goes home.
Alone at last: my dad, me
And my mother's ghost.

NAP

I turn down the old faded pink-checkered spread
and tuck myself into my small childhood bed
then sleep for three hours and wake up with dread
unsure if my mother is downstairs or dead

MISSED BY

The chair near the window its back and seat cold
The shawl that no longer has shoulders to hold

The black purse you held like a cat in your lap
The side of the bed where you no longer nap

The wooden mezzuzah you hung by the door
The red and gold rug that you hooked for the floor

The cup marked "The Boss" which you drank from each night
The tea and the sugar know something's not right

The telephone pines for the sound of your laugh
The tub longs to draw you a warm sudsy bath

The kitchen you ruled with your big wooden spoon
Is holding out hope you'll return to us soon

Unable to take in the news of your death
Your house sits on tenterhooks holding its breath

SITTING SHIVA

Mirrors are covered
Wooden benches are set out
Have a good mourning

Where's the coffee pot?
I ask my father, who knows
my mother would know

Welcome. Please come in.
Sit anywhere. Except there!
That's my mother's chair

Ancient Hebrew prayers
cannot bring my mother back,
so what good are they?

My aunt spills her tea
when I speak to her softly
in my mother's voice

White coffee cup smeared
with my mother's red lipstick.
Don't you dare wash it.

Chocolate rugelach
my mother and I both love
clog my throat like mud

My mother's old friend
cups my face with wilted hands
Fingers wet with tears

My aunt stands to leave.
"Call if you need anything."
I need my mother.

ONE MORE THING

My mother crept downstairs at night,
(I made believe I was asleep)
She didn't bother with the light,
Her need for solitude ran deep.

She smoked a cigarette or two,
She drank a tepid cup of tea
And then with nothing left to do,
At last she let herself just be.

For hours lost in thought she sat
The kitchen quiet as a grave,
Was she content or sorry that
for years she gave and gave and gave?

I missed my chance to ask her so,
That's one more thing I'll never know.

AT NIGHT

Sorrow takes me to bed at night
Limbs as heavy as lead at night
Clutched in the arms of dread at night
Holding on by a thread at night
Books on the stand unread at night
Tears on the pillow shed at night
Hearing the things she said at night
Her voice alive in my head at night
Regret and remorse widespread at night
Guilt and "if onlys" fed at night
Peace and relief are shred at night
Panic and worry are wed at night
To be anywhere else instead at night
I sleep the sleep of the dead at night

STOPPING BY DREAMS ON A LONELY EVENING

Whose face this is I think I know,
I recognize from long ago.
My mother, can it really be?
For days on end I've missed her so.

For nights on end, so desperately
I've shut my eyes in hopes to see
My mother smiling with delight
And reaching out her hand to me.

She floats by in a shroud of white
And whispers, "Hush now, I'm all right.
You promised me you wouldn't weep."
And then she disappears from sight.

My dream is lovely, dark and deep
And I've a promise now to keep,
And years to hold her in my sleep
And years to hold her in my sleep.

BEACON

Cold dark wintry night
Who will light the way for me?
The mom in the moon

LOST ART

The art of losing my mother is hard to master;
Like a little girl in the woods who can't find her way,
I'm afraid I will never survive this disaster.

Of course, somewhere inside I knew I would outlast her,
Though I did all I could to keep that notion at bay.
The art of losing my mother is hard to master.

She might return. Who knows? I wouldn't put it past her.
Denial is not a river in Egypt, they say,
but it is one way to get me through this disaster.

As days slip by, the distance between us grows vaster,
my fading memories add to my growing dismay.
The art of losing my mother is hard to master.

Surely God made a great mistake when he miscast her
as Dead Mother, a role she was never meant to play
in the movie of my life, now called "The Disaster."

If time heals all wounds, can't it do so any faster?
Though I never did believe in that tired cliché.
The art of losing my mother is too hard to master,
I cannot get a grip on this crippling disaster.

SO LONG

So long
between the day
she took her final breath
and the day we laid her to rest
So long

MY MOTHER WOULD NOT STOP FOR DEATH

My Mother would not stop for Death
And so He stopped, for She
Was ready for that final Breath—
And eager to be Free.

Death pulled into the Parking Lot
And climbed the Narrow Stair—
To find the room that Time forgot—
My Mother waited there.

In sleek black tux, Top Hat and shoes
More Handsome than a Groom,
A gent Nobody could Refuse—
Death strode into the Room.

And though My Mother lay abed,
Death swept her off her Feet,
In one swift moment they were Wed—
My Mother's life Complete.

The Couple hastened out the Door
He held her by the Hand,
Now she and Death—her Paramour—
Dwell in the Promised Land.

That morning was so Long Ago,
Yet feels like Yesterday,
When Death became My Mother's Beau—
And stole her straight away.

SPRING

Look!
Hey Dad!
The garden!
The hyacinths!
Aren't they gorgeous!
Don't they smell like heaven?
Dew spills from my father's eyes.
Your mother loved those flowers so.
When I saw them spring up from the ground
My broken heart   broke all over again.

WHO HAS SEEN MY MOM?

Who has seen my mom?
Neither I nor you:
But when my dad bows down his head
My mom is passing through.

Who has seen my mom?
Neither you nor I:
But when my eyes well up with tears,
My mom is passing by.

NEARBY

My mother
is far
away
as can be
and
always
as close
as my heart
is to me

WISH LIST

What I Wouldn't Give To See My Mother One More Time:

YAHRZEIT

Golden autumn leaves
drift lazily through the air
onto Mother's grave

White winter snowflakes
fall all over themselves to
blanket Mother's grave

Gentle spring raindrops
are sent down from the heavens
to wash Mother's grave

Warm summer breezes
chase pale yellow butterflies
around Mother's grave

Today marks a year
endless tears soak one small stone
placed on Mother's grave

Epilogue: Wherever I Go

I CARRY MY MOTHER

I carry my mother wherever I go
Her belly, her thighs, her plentiful hips
Her milky white skin she called this side of snow
The crease of her brow and the plump of her lips

Her belly, her thighs, her plentiful hips
The curl of her hair and her sharp widow's peak
The crease of her brow and the plump of her lips
The hook of her nose and the curve of her cheek

The curl of her hair and her sharp widow's peak
The dark beauty mark to the left of her chin
The hook of her nose and the curve of her cheek
Her delicate wrist so impossibly thin

The dark beauty mark to the left of her chin
Her deep set brown eyes that at times appeared black
Her delicate wrist so impossibly thin
I stare at the mirror, my mother stares back

Her deep set brown eyes that at times appeared black
Her milky white skin she called this side of snow
I stare at the mirror, my mother stares back
I carry my mother wherever I go

Notes

p. 25   "Thirteen Ways of Looking at My Mother" was inspired by "Thirteen Ways of Looking at a Blackbird" by Wallace Stevens from *The Collected Poems of Wallace Stevens* (New York: Knopf, 1954).

p. 36   "Pills" was inspired by *One Fish Two Fish Red Fish Blue Fish* by Dr. Seuss (New York: Random House, 1960).

p. 46   "How to Watch Your Mother Die," was inspired by "How to watch your brother die" by Michael Lassell from Decade Dance (Boston: Alyson Books, 1990).

p. 49   "Prayer" was inspired by "Do not go gentle into that good night" by Dylan Thomas from *The Poems of Dylan Thomas* (New York: New Directions, 1939).

p. 52   "How to Watch Your Father Watch Your Mother Die" was inspired by "How to watch your brother die" by Michael Lassell from *Decade Dance* (Boston: Alyson Books, 1990).

p. 57   "Letter from Mom, Postmarked Heaven" was inspired by "This Is Just to Say" by William Carlos Williams, from *The Collected Poems of William Carlos Williams* (New York: New Directions, 1938).

p. 58   "Looking at Her" was inspired by "Looking at Each Other" by Muriel Rukeyser from *Breaking Open* (Random House, 1973).

p. 59   "How to Bury Your Mother" was inspired by "How to visit the grave of a friend" by Michael Lassell from *Decade Dance* (Boston: Alyson Books, 1990).

p. 61   "My Mother Has My Heart" was inspired by "My True Love Hath My Heart" by Sir Philip Sidney, written in the 1500's.

p. 68   "At Night" was inspired by "Of Night" by Molly Peacock from *The Second Blush* (New York: Norton, 2008).

p. 69   "Stopping By Dreams on a Lonely Evening" was inspired by "Stopping by Woods on a Snowy Evening" by Robert Frost from *The Poetry of Robert Frost* (New York: Henry Holt and Company, 1923, 1969).

p. 71   "Lost Art" was inspired by "One Art" by Elizabeth Bishop from *The Complete Poems, 1926-1979* (New York: Farrar, Straus & Giroux, 1979, 1983).

p. 73   "My Mother Would Not Stop for Death" was inspired by "Because I could not stop for Death" by Emily Dickinson, written in the 1800's.

p. 76   "Who Has Seen My Mom?" was inspired by "Who Has Seen the Wind?" by Christina Rossetti, written in the 1800's.

p. 77   "Nearby" was inspired by "Proximity" by Gregory Corso, from *Herald of the Autochthonic Spirit* (New York: New Directions, 1981).

p. 78   "Wish List" was inspired by "Empty List Poem" by Meg Kearney from *The Secret of Me: A Novel in Poems* (New York: Persea Books, 2005).

Acknowledgements

Grateful acknowledgement is made to the editors of the following publications in which these poems, sometimes in earlier versions, first appeared:

Big Scream: "Soon"

Adrienne: A Poetry Journal of Queer Women: "Safe Passage," "How to Bury Your Mother," I Carry My Mother," and "Thirteen Ways of Looking at My Mother"

At Length Magazine: "The Deal"

Lavender Review: "Looking at Her"

Meat for Tea: The Valley Review: "A Daughter's a Daughter," "My Mother Would Not Stop For Death," "Pills," and "The Problem"

Mom Egg Review: "In the ICU"

The Louisville Review: "My Mother Is"

Festival Writer: Sestinas: "When Things Fall Apart"

The author offers heartfelt thanks and boundless gratitude to Risa Denenberg and Mary Meriam of Headmistress Press; Elizabeth Harding and Stuart Waterman of Curtis Brown, Ltd.; cover artist Carol Marine; first readers Plynn Gutman, Helena Kriel, Ellen LaFlèche, Eleanor Morse, and Baron Wormser; writing group members Corinne Demas, Barbara Diamond Goldin, Patty MacLachlan, Ann Turner, Ellen Wittlinger, and Jane Yolen; friends and family members who were there when needed (too many to mention; you know who you are); and Mary Grace Newman Vazquez, my guiding light and shining star.

Photo by Mary Vazquez

About the Author

Lesléa Newman is the author of 70 books for readers of all ages including the poetry collections, *Still Life with Buddy, Nobody's Mother,* and *Signs of Love,* and the novel-in-verse, *October Mourning: A Song for Matthew Shepard.* Ms. Newman has received many literary awards including poetry fellowships from the National Endowment for the Arts and the Massachusetts Artists Foundation, and a Stonewall Honor from the American Library Association. Her poetry has been published in *Spoon River Poetry Review, Cimarron Review, Columbia: A Journal of Literature and Art, Evergreen Chronicles, Harvard Gay and Lesbian Review, Lilith Magazine, Kalliope, The Sun, Bark Magazine, Sow's Ear Poetry Review, Seventeen Magazine* and others. Nine of her books have been Lambda Literary Award Finalists. From 2008-2010 she served as the poet laureate of Northampton, Massachusetts. Currently she lives in Holyoke, Massachusetts and is a faculty member of Spalding University's low-residency MFA in Writing program.

Made in the USA
Middletown, DE
14 September 2019